Cattitude

BY DANE BJORKLUND

Scholastic Inc.

Dedicated to Roscoe and Rue

Photos ©: cover top: Hulya Ozkok/Rex Features/AP Images; cover bottom left: Courtesy Waffles the Cat; cover bottom center: (@cobythecat) CB2/ZOB/Supplied by WENN/Newscom; cover bottom right: @venustwofacecat; 1 top: Barcroft Media/Getty Images; 1 bottom: Michael Stewart/Getty Images; 3 top: Hulya Ozkok/Rex Features/AP Images; 3 center: Barcroft Media/Getty Images; 3 bottom: Michael and Deirdre Cross; 4 left: Janet Mayer/Splash News/Newscom; 4 right: CB2/ZOB/Supplied by WENN.com/Newscom; 5 top left: Hulya Ozkok/Rex Features/AP Images; 5 top right: Q-Images/Alamy Stock Photo; 5 bottom: Chris Carlson/AP Images; 6: David Livingston/Getty Images; 7: Bret Hartman for Friskies/AP Images; 8: halbergman/Getty Images; 9 left: Araya Diaz/Getty Images; 9 right: Mark Von Holden/AP Images for Discovery Communications; 10, 11: @venustwofacecat; 12: Courtesy Waffles the Cat; 13 left: Janet Mayer/Splash News/Newscom; 13 right: Amy Sussman/AP Images for Friskies; 14, 15: Europics/Newscom; 16: CB2/ZOB/Supplied by WENN/Newscom; 17 top: mitry Kaminsky/Dreamstime; 17 bottom left, bottom right: CB2/ZOB/Supplied by WENN/Newscom; 18, 19: Cole & Marmalade - coleandmarmalade.com; 20: Rex Features/AP Images; 21: Barcroft Media/Getty Images; 22: Hulya Ozkok/Rex Features/AP Images; 23 top: Andreykuzmin/Dreamstime; 23 bottom left, bottom right: Hulya Ozkok/Rex Features/AP Images; 24: Meow Quarterly/Rex Shutterstock/AP Images; 25 top: Tonympix/Dreamstime; 25 bottom: Meow Quarterly/Rex Shutterstock/AP Images; 26, 27 left: Q-Images/Alamy Stock Photo; 27 right: Richard Anderson/Getty Images; 28, 29: Matt Rourke/AP Images; 30: CB2/ZOB/Supplied by WENN/Newscom; 31 top: Melbyika/Dreamstime; 31 bottom left, bottom right: CB2/ZOB/Supplied by WENN/Newscom; 32, 33: Jessie Jones; 34, 35: Courtesy of Jason Scott; 36, 37: Miyoko Ihara/Rex Features/AP Images; 38, 39: Barcroft Media/Getty Images; 40, 41 left: Richard Vogel/AP Images; 41 right: CB2/ZOB/Supplied by WENN/Newscom; 42: Dwayne Senior/Newscom; 43: Neale Haynes/Getty Images; 44, 45: ZJAN/www.facebook.com/blindcathoneybe/Newscom; 46, 47: Michael and Deirdre Cross.

ISBN 978-1-338-11148-4

10 9 8 7 6 5 4 3 2   16 17 18 19 20

Printed in the U.S.A.   40

First printing 2016

mojo media

Book design by Mojo Media Inc.
Director, Joe Funk; Art Director, Daniel Tideman

All social media numbers included in this book are accurate as of the publication date.

Cat Contents

GARFI

ALBERT

COOPER

WAFFLES

DIDGA

Welcome to the exciting and adorable world of Internet cats!

What you'll find inside the pages ahead are many of the most interesting and famous cats in the world, and they've all achieved their stardom from sharing pictures, videos, and stories online. Many of these cats were the runts of their litters, most were rescued from shelters around the world, and all of them have huge personalities and even bigger online followings. With a parent's permission, you can check out your favorites on Facebook, Instagram, Twitter, and YouTube.

Meow let's get started!

WINSTON SMUSHFACE

TUNA

Did you know that in the United States roughly 33 percent of all households have a pet cat? That's more than 75 million pet cats! **Every year 1.3 million cats are adopted from shelters in the US.** If you're a cat lover, ask a parent to contact a local shelter and find out ways that you can volunteer. Even if you're not ready to have a pet, there are plenty of ways to help cats in need!

COLONEL MEOW

One look at Colonel Meow and you'll know exactly why he's such a big deal on the Internet. His piercing yellow eyes, fierce snarl, and Guinness World Record nine-inch-long fur have made the Colonel an Internet sensation and the subject of fan art from admirers around the world. "The Angriest Cat in the World," as he's been referred to, first became famous in 2012 after his pictures were uploaded to The Daily What. Since then he's appeared on BuzzFeed, the Huffington Post, and CNN's *Anderson Live*.

CAT FACTS

Breed	Himalayan-Persian
Owner	Anne Marie Avery
Hometown	Los Angeles, California
Facebook Fans	507,000
First Internet Appearance	The Daily What, 2012
Claim to Fame	2014 Guinness World Record for cat with the longest fur (9 inches!)

Q: What's the difference between a cat and a comma?

A: One has claws at the end of its paws, the other is a pause at the end of a clause!

The All-Stars
The most famous of them all!

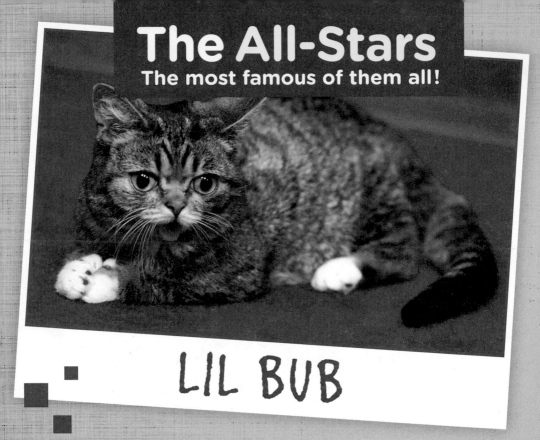

LIL BUB

Her enormous green eyes, constantly hanging-out tongue, and extra digit on each paw are just a few of the characteristics that make Lil BUB so special. In 2011, Mike Bridavsky—already the owner of four rescue cats—went to visit the runt of a feral cat's litter in rural Indiana. When Mike picked up the kitten, he exclaimed, "Hey, bub!" and the rest is history. Lil BUB's distinct look is a result of several genetic mutations including feline dwarfism, an undeveloped lower jaw, and a rare bone condition called osteopetrosis. Despite these setbacks, BUB is an extremely happy and loving cat. She has helped raise over $200,000 for special needs pets, has appeared on *Good Morning America*, the *Today* show, and *The View*, and she was even the subject of an award-winning documentary, *Lil BUB & Friendz*.

> "IN ANCIENT TIMES CATS WERE WORSHIPED AS GODS; THEY HAVE NOT FORGOTTEN THIS."
> — Terry Pratchett

CAT FACTS

Hometown	Bloomington, Indiana
Owner	Mike Bridavsky
Favorite Food	Yogurt
Facebook Fans	2.9 million
Instagram Followers	1.3 million @iamlilbub
Music Career	In 2015, Lil BUB released a full-length album titled *Science and Magic*.

VENUS

When Christina and Chris—the owners of one orange tabby cat and one black tuxedo cat—saw a Facebook picture of a stray two-faced cat, they knew they had to have her. The Florida residents flew to North Carolina, where they first met Venus, perhaps the most genetically mysterious (and beautiful!) cat on the Internet. Feline geneticists have suggested two possible causes for Venus's split coat. One theory identifies Venus as a chimera, the result of two zygotes (and therefore two sets of DNA) fusing together. The other theory: complete luck!

CAT FACTS

Coat Color	Tortoiseshell
Eye Color	One green, one blue
Hometown	Florida
Facebook Fans	1.3 million
Tagline	0% Photoshopped 100% Born This Way!
Instagram Followers	973,000 @Venustwofacecat

FUN FACT

Cats have thirty-two muscles in their ears. That's twenty-six more than humans have!

The Cuddlers
The softest, friendliest of the bunch

WAFFLES

Owners (and former dog people) Derek Liu and Laine Lee liken the story of their adorable cat Waffles to that of the ugly duckling. Waffles was the runt and last remaining kitten of her litter when the couple showed up at a shelter just to look around. The tiny six-month-old kitten began licking their hands and they knew they had to have her. Laine shared lots of pictures with friends and family on Facebook and before she knew it, Waffles was racking up thousands of likes. Perhaps Waffles's most famous pic shows her poking her head through a piece of bread.

CAT FACTS

Breed	Scottish Fold
Hometown	California
Owners	Derek Liu and Laine Lee
Facebook Fans	2.4 million
Hobbies	Paper bags, cardboard, and feathers
Claim to Fame	One of *Cosmopolitan*'s 50 Most Fascinating People on the Internet

SNOOPY

It's difficult to tell from looking at photographs if Snoopy is a real cat or actually just a stuffed animal. His big brown eyes, perfectly groomed soft coat, and fluffy ringed tail make him perhaps the cutest cat on the Internet. Snoopy, who lives in the Sichuan province of China, began his adventure toward cyberspace stardom when his owner created an account on the Chinese social network Weibo. Fans from around the world have since launched several tribute accounts to Snoopy on Tumblr, Instagram, and Facebook.

CAT FACTS

Full Name	Snoopybabe
Hometown	Sichuan, China
Birthday	May 11, 2011
Owner	Miss Ning
Breed	Exotic Shorthair
Instagram Followers	332,000 @snoopybabe

Q:

What's the unluckiest kind of cat to have?

A:

A catastrophe!

COBY

Coby's mesmerizing big blue eyes might just be the most stunning cat eyes on the Internet. Most cats lose their blue kitten eyes as they grow up, but Coby's have stayed the same glowing shade of blue since birth. And Coby's eyes aren't the only thing that make her stand out; her perfectly white coat and playful personality are Internet gold. Coby, who is a British Shorthair, has even been known to dress up for holidays and special events.

CAT FACTS

Breed	British Shorthair
Owner	Rebecca Schefkind
Hometown	Baltimore, Maryland
Favorite Food	Tuna!
Facebook Fans	100,000
Instagram Followers	538,000 @cobythecat

COLE AND MARMALADE

Not only are Cole and Marmalade (Marm for short) best friends, they're also both rescue kitties and award-winning YouTube celebrities! Owner Chris Poole has been a lifelong self-proclaimed crazy cat guy. He even spent seven years working with lions, tigers, and other exotic cats in Florida. Today, Poole and wife, Jessica Josephs, regularly upload videos of Cole and Marmalade to YouTube and watch the views stack up. Their videos frequently promote cat adoption and care.

Cole with owner Chris Poole

CAT FACTS

Breed	**Cole: Turkish Angora (most likely)** **Marmalade: short-haired ginger tabby**
Owner	**Chris Poole and Jessica Josephs**
Birthday	**Cole: March 1, 2012 (estimated)** **Marmalade: July 1, 2013**
Hometown	**Oceanside, California**
YouTube	**334,000 subscribers** **86 million views**
Instagram Followers	**118,000 @coleandmarmalade**

19

The Mystics
The most interesting-looking cats on the Internet

SAM

Sam's constantly furrowed eyebrows make him the most concerned-looking cat on the Internet. But don't worry, this kitty's nervous appearance doesn't reflect his curious and playful personality. Sam was discovered abandoned in 2012, but his worried look wasn't immediately noticed. When one of owner Amanda Collado's friends pointed out Sam's expressive eyebrows, she decided to make him his own Instagram account.

CAT FACTS

Owner	Amanda Collado
Hometown	New York, New York
Favorite Food	Tomatoes
Look-alikes	Martin Scorsese, Groucho Marx
Facebook Fans	504,000
Instagram Followers	193,000 @samhaseyebrows

? DID YOU KNOW?

The ridges on a cat's nose are as unique as human fingerprints.

GARFI

What truly makes Garfi stand out on the Internet is not only his constant glare, but also the beautiful photographs owner Hulya Ozkok takes to document his everyday adventures. Ozkok, a professional photographer in Istanbul, loves to dress her cat Garfi in joyful, bright costumes to contrast with his sinister appearance. The result: Internet gold. Garfi has racked up thousands of fans on social media and several articles, including write-ups in the Huffington Post, *USA Today*, and the *Daily Mail*.

CAT FACTS

Breed	Persian
Owner	Hulya Ozkok
Hometown	Istanbul, Turkey
Facebook Fans	106,000
Instagram Followers	62,000 @meetgarfi
First Internet Appearance	Flickr, 2010

PRINCESS MONSTER TRUCK

Artists Tracy Timmons and Joseph Bryce were walking to their home in Brooklyn, New York, one night when a creature jumped out of a bush and landed at their feet. After a moment of investigation it became clear that this thing before them was a cat—a very, very special cat. Princess Monster Truck's glowing yellow eyes, long fur, and extreme underbite make her one of the most unusual-looking cats on the Internet. Timmons and Bryce began posting pictures of PMT to an Instagram account for their jewelry line, but followers quickly began asking for more of the cat.

CAT FACTS

Breed	Persian
Owners	Tracy Timmons and Joseph Bryce
Hometown	Brooklyn, New York
Nicknames	Monster, PMT
Hobbies	Chillin', heavy metal
Instagram Followers	235,000 @princessmonstertruck

TUNA AND THE ROCK CATS

Samantha Martin's multitalented musical act the Rock Cats are not only the only cat band in existence, but also the greatest cat band in existence! Led by front-cat and cowbell player Tuna, this exciting band is made up of six rescued cats, a chicken named Cluck Norris, and, occasionally, a gong-playing groundhog named Garfield. Every great band has an awesome tour bus and the Rock Cats are no different. Martin's team just raised over $150,000 on Kickstarter to upgrade their bus and tour the country!

CAT FACTS

Owner/Trainer	Samantha Martin
Hometown	Chicago, Illinois
Members	Tuna, OZ, Dakota, Asti, Nue, Sookie, Garfield Gong, and Cluck
Music Genre	Freeform Jazz
Facebook Fans	9,400
Inspirations	Alice Cooper and catnip

Q:

What did one cat say to the other cat while chewing on a DVD?

A:

The book was better.

NORA

It took a year of patiently watching her owner Betsy Alexander give piano lessons before Nora the cat decided to jump up on the bench and start playing. Since her initial tapping, Nora, who was adopted by Betsy Alexander and Burnell Yow of Philadelphia, Pennsylvania, in 2006, has learned how to play multiple notes at once, how to play high notes and low notes (she likes the high notes much more), and even how to play duets with Betsy and her human students. Videos of Nora's improvisational skills have been viewed more than ten million times on YouTube!

CAT FACTS

Coat Color	Gray Tabby
Owners	Betsy Alexander and Burnell Yow
Hometown	Philadelphia, Pennsylvania
Named After	Artist and writer Leonora Carrington
Facebook Fans	21,000
YouTube Views	More than 10 million

"I had been told that the training procedure with cats was difficult. It's not. Mine had me trained in two days."
— Bill Dana

DIDGA

Whether she's surfing, skateboarding, or doing gymnastics, Didga is certainly the most active and talented cat on the Internet. So how did Didga learn all of these incredible skills? Lots and lots of practice. Owner Robert Dollwet is a professional dog trainer who decided to try teaching his cat Didga a few tricks after adopting her from a shelter in Australia at thirteen months old. Didga eventually caught on to Dollwet's method and can now even use and flush a human toilet!

CAT FACTS

Coat Color	Tabby
Owner	Robert Dollwet
Hometown	Gold Coast, Australia
Full Name	Didgeridoo
YouTube Views	43 million
Facebook Video Views	More than 90 million

Q:

Why don't cats play poker in the jungle?

A:

Too many cheetahs!

WINSTON SMUSHFACE

Jessie Jones, a self-described dog person, knew she had stumbled upon something special as soon as she met Winston Smushface. Jessie and her partner, Nick Atkins, found Winston at a breeder after he was returned by a woman who could no longer take care of him. Winston now has his own Instagram account where he's constantly sticking out his tongue and striking his signature pose: sitting like a human. News anchors on Australia's *Today* show had a difficult time getting through an interview with Winston because they couldn't stop laughing.

CAT FACTS

Full Name:	**Sir Winston Smushface**
Hometown	**Gold Coast, Australia**
Instagram Followers	**18,000 @winstonsmushface**
Owners:	**Nick Atkins and Jessie Jones**
Breed:	**Peke-faced Persian**
Hobbies:	**Chilling out, sitting like a human**

SOCKINGTON

Sockington the cat, also sometimes known as Socks and Sockamillion, totally dominates the social network Twitter with more than 1.3 million followers. This handsome domestic shorthair was originally discovered outside of a subway station in Boston, Massachusetts, before being adopted by Jason Scott of Waltham, Massachusetts. Scott launched Sockington's Twitter career in 2007, and began gaining five hundred to five thousand new followers a day after being added to Twitter's list of recommended feeds in 2009.

CAT FACTS

Owner	Jason Scott
Hometown	Waltham, Massachusetts
Nicknames	Socks, Sockamillion
Facebook Fans	353,000
Twitter Followers	1.36 million @sockington

? DID YOU KNOW?

Cats spend 70 percent of their lives sleeping. That's a lot of cat naps.

Fukumaru and
owner Misao Ihara

FUKUMARU

Fukumaru and his ninety-two-year-old owner, Misao Ihara (better known Misao the Big Mama), can certainly be described as the sweetest pet and owner pair on the Internet. Misao discovered the small white kitten in a barn on her property in the Chiba Prefecture of Japan and the two instantly became best friends. Fukumaru—which means "good fortune"—never left Misao's side, even when working long hours on her farm. Their epic friendship has been documented by Misao's granddaughter Miyoko and published in a book appropriately titled *Misao The Big Mama and Fukumaru the Cat.*

CAT FACTS

"WHAT GREATER GIFT THAN THE LOVE OF A CAT."
— Charles Dickens

Owner	Misao the Big Mama
Hometown	Chiba, Japan
Photographer	Miyoko Ihara
Eye Coloring	One yellow, one blue
Facebook Fans	15,000
Hobbies	Farming, going everywhere with Misao

ALBERT

His enormous wardrobe and influential Outfit of the Day (#OOTD) selections make Albert Baby Cat one of the most stylish and fashion-forward cats on the Internet. Albert, who was named after Albert Einstein, has been photographed in everything from a three-piece suit to his favorite ducky bathrobe. Where does Albert get all of his stylish new threads? Owner and photographer Christine Look pieces them together from doll outfits and dog costumes. Look hopes that one day Albert's Instagram success will be able to launch him to the big screen!

CAT FACTS

Breed	Munchkin
Full Name	Albert Baby Cat
Owners	Christine Look and Sandeep Gupta
Hometown	Los Angeles, California
Instagram Followers	350,000 @albertbabycat
Favorite Foods	Bananas and dry seaweed

? DID YOU KNOW?
Most female cats are right-pawed while most male cats are left-pawed.

The Professionals
The most skilled cats around

TARA

"Heroic" and "loyal" aren't words typically used to describe cats; however, Tara isn't your typical cat. In 2014, four-year-old Jeremy Triantafilo was playing in his family's driveway in Bakersfield, California, when a neighbor's dog suddenly attacked the young child. As soon as the dog got hold of Jeremy's leg, Tara, the family's cat, sprung to action, pouncing on the dog and defending her owner. Video of Tara's heroic feat quickly went viral on YouTube and the Triantafilos' cat has since received several awards and honors for her courage, including throwing out the first pitch at a baseball game. The Bakersfield Board of Supervisors even declared June 3 as Tara the Hero Cat Day!

Tara with the Triantafilo family.

CAT FACTS

Full Name	Zatara
Nickname	Tara the Hero Cat
Owners	The Triantafilo family
Hometown	Bakersfield, California
YouTube Views	26.7 million
Facebook Fans	44,000

? DID YOU KNOW?

Most cats can run up to thirty miles per hour. That's three miles per hour faster than Olympian Usain Bolt.

 41

The Professionals
The most skilled cats around

BOB

Bob the Street Cat's now-giant career began very humbly in Tottenham, London, in 2007. James Bowen, a local street musician, was walking home one night when he stumbled upon an injured orange cat. Bowen took the cat to a vet to have his wounds treated and then began trying to find his owner. No owner was found, and Bowen realized this cat, who he named Bob, wouldn't leave his side. Bowen brought Bob along on his busking adventures around London, and eventually crowds gathered to watch and support the musician and his cat. Bob and Bowen have since published seven books and a movie is currently in the works to share their story.

CAT FACTS

Owner	James Bowen
Hometown	London, England
Nickname	Street Cat Bob
Facebook Fans	465,000
Twitter Followers	79,000 @streetcatbob
Best Celebrity Encounters	Paul McCartney and Rupert Grint

Q:
What's a cat's favorite color?

A:
Purrrrrrple!

Bob and owner James Bowen

HONEY BEE

If you find yourself out exploring the hiking trails of the Caribbean Islands, you just might bump into an adventurous and brave blind cat named Honey Bee. Owner Sabrina Ursin first saw Honey Bee while volunteering at the Animals Fiji shelter at the beginning of a vacation. Ursin met several animals on her many volunteering adventures, but when she met Honey Bee in Fiji, she knew she had to have her. Honey Bee first started out exploring Ursin's yard and getting used to being on a leash. Eventually she built up the skills to take on some hiking trails in the Pacific Northwest. Despite her inability to see, Honey Bee uses her other senses to explore and detect when cliffs and ledges are near.

CAT FACTS

Owners	Sabrina Ursin
Hometown	The Caribbean Islands
Discovered	Animals Fiji shelter
Favorite Hike	Mason Lake near Seattle, Washington
YouTube Views	1.1 million
Facebook Fans	26,000

Q:
Why do cats always get their way?

A:
They're very purrsuasive!

The Professionals
The most skilled cats around

COOPER

Most cats are known for sleeping, scratching, and sitting in boxes—not Cooper. Once a week, Cooper the cat gets a small digital camera strapped onto his collar and roams the streets and parks of Seattle capturing beautiful images of everything from sunsets to alley cats. Cooper's camera snaps a picture once every two minutes during his weekly adventures. You can check out some of Cooper's best shots on his website, or pick up a copy of his own book, *Cat Cam.*

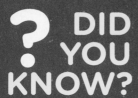
CAT FACTS

Breed	American Shorthair
Owners	Michael and Deirdre Cross
Hometown	Seattle, Washington
Birthday	September 17, 2005
Facebook Fans	991,000
Website	PhotographerCat.com

Feline Photo Fun!

① ### Get a cat (if you don't have one already)!
There are tons of awesome feline friends waiting for you at local shelters. Have a parent help you find a nearby location and schedule a visit.

② ### Find a camera.
Any camera will do.

③ ### Have fun and get creative!
Try to capture your cat's best moments, from silly to sweet.

Does your furry friend sleep in hilarious positions, or is he willing to tolerate kitty costumes? Keep your cat's comfort level in mind, and always have that camera handy for spontaneous moments of cuteness!